PO
PUB

# The Cotswolds

**Nigel Vile**

COUNTRYSIDE BOOKS
NEWBURY BERKSHIRE

First published 2011


COUNTRYSIDE BOOKS
3 Catherine Road
Newbury, Berkshire

To view our complete range of books,
please visit us at
www.countrysidebooks.co.uk

ISBN 978 1 84674 226 2

Cover photograph of Castle Combe by Bernard Humphries
supplied by Pictures of Britain
Photograph on page 1 courtesy of Mike Plant

Designed by Peter Davies, Nautilus Design
Produced through MRM Associates Ltd., Reading
Typeset by CJWT Solutions, St Helens
Printed in India

# Contents

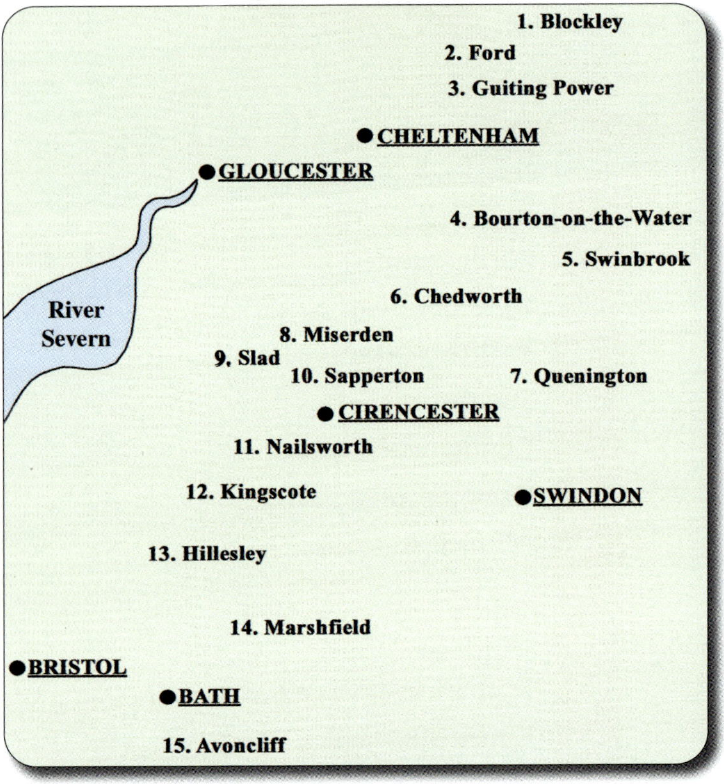


*Area map showing location of the walks*

# Introduction

What better way to spend a leisurely few hours than to stretch your legs and then visit a traditional pub for a delicious meal or snack and a glass of beer or wine? The fifteen circular walks in this book allow you to do just that. Each route takes you through some of the finest scenery in the Cotswolds Area of Outstanding Natural Beauty.

The Cotswolds conjure up a range of different images, but the overriding impression is of classic English landscape as typified in any number of picture postcards and calendars ... sheltered valleys, stone cottages alongside charming rivers, magnificent churches founded upon the prosperity of the woollen trade, and the high wolds with sheep grazing pasture. The place-names read like a geographical *Who's Who* – Bourton-on-the-Water, the Slaughters, Chedworth, Slad and Bibury being just a few of the villages featured. The list of romantic-sounding places seems almost endless. These golden stone towns and villages have appeared in so many glossy books and television programmes that the view at every turn appears vaguely familiar or even commonplace, even to the first-time visitor.

With the area justifiably popular with so many people in today's mobile age, the tourist honeypots can become busy and crowded. The best way to appreciate and enjoy this most English of landscapes, therefore, is to literally set out on foot and forsake the village centres – hence this book of walks.

All the routes are between 3 and 6½ miles in length. Car parking options have been suggested in the vicinity of each pub, although in many cases it will be possible to park at the hostelry itself. If doing this, please seek the publican's permission before setting off on your walk and promise to return for a meal and a drink afterwards. A sketch map, indicating the route to be followed, accompanies each walk. However, I would always recommend carrying the relevant OS Explorer or Outdoor Leisure map as well – these are as vital a part of the walker's kit as sturdy boots and a rucksack.

Places of interest close to each walk are suggested should you have a few hours to spare, and don't forget to carry a snack and a drink in that trustworthy rucksack, as well as a decent set of waterproofs. Despite occasional belief to the contrary, the authors of walking guidebooks cannot guarantee their readers sunny weather! And remember that rain creates muddy paths, and no publican wants a trail of mud through the lounge or public bar – do attempt some form of wash and brush-up before entering these fine inns.

It just remains for me to wish you many happy hours of pleasure in following these pub walks.

**Nigel Vile**

***Footnote:*** If you have any problems with any of these walks, do not hesitate to contact me on vilewalks@yahoo.co.uk and any amendments will then be posted on the vilewalks Facebook pages to help other readers.

---

# Publisher's Note

We hope that you obtain considerable enjoyment from this book; great care has been taken in its preparation. However, changes of landlord and actual closures are sadly not uncommon. Likewise, although at the time of publication all routes followed public rights of way or permitted paths, diversion orders can be made and permissions withdrawn.

We cannot, of course, be held responsible for such diversion orders and any inaccuracies in the text which result from these or any other changes to the routes nor any damage which might result from walkers trespassing on private property. We are anxious though that all details covering the walks are kept up to date and would therefore welcome information from readers which would be relevant to future editions.

The simple sketch maps that accompany the walks in this book are based on notes made by the author whilst checking out the routes on the ground. However, for the benefit of a proper map, we do recommend that you purchase the relevant Ordnance Survey sheet covering your walk. The Ordnance Survey maps are widely available, especially through booksellers and local newsagents.

POCKET PUB WALKS

# 1 Blockley

## *The Crown Inn*

**As with so many Cotswold villages**, it was the textile trade and mills that contributed to much of Blockley's wealth. The village was built on the steep slopes of a hollow beneath the high wolds, close to the head of what has been described as a 'small but prolific' stream. At one time, there were no fewer than six silk mills in this little place that provided much of the silk required by Coventry's ribbon manufacturers. Across the fields from Blockley lies Batsford, a tidy estate village at the

**Distance** – 4 miles.

**OS Outdoor Leisure** 45 The Cotswolds. GR SP163348. A steep climb out of Blockley onto the hilltops above the village; otherwise, a gently undulating landscape.

**Starting point** The Crown Inn at Blockley.

***How to get there*** *Take the A44 and turn off 2 miles west of Moreton-in-Marsh to follow the B4479 into Blockley. In the village, turn into the street signposted to the village centre. In 250 yards, this will bring you to the Crown Inn. Park with consideration in the vicinity of the pub.*

entrance to Batsford Park. The neo-Tudor mansion and neo-Norman church will catch the eye, whilst a visit to the arboretum – see below – is worth combining with this walk. Between Blockley and Batsford lies a delightful pastoral landscape, typical of the northern wolds. There are steep inclines, ancient woodland and far-ranging views, the most memorable of which comes towards journey's end. As the path emerges from Park Plantation onto high open ground there is a delightful outlook across towards Blockley, with its streets, terraces and houses clinging to the distant hillside.

THE PUB The **Crown Inn**, located at the end of Blockley's High Street, is a former coaching inn dating from 1574. Its golden stone walls and Virginia creeper present a handsome exterior to the visitor, who will find the interior equally pleasing. Old beams, open fireplaces, a fine restaurant and a comfortable lounge make for a most relaxing atmosphere. Excellent snacks and real ales are available in the bar area, although on a warm summer's day the former cobbled courtyard will no doubt prove a temptation. Now a patio area, this is quite the perfect place to rest and linger with tea or coffee and a newspaper.

*The Crown Inn is also a hotel and is open all day. ☎ 01386 700245; postcode: GL56 9EX; www.crowninncotswolds.co.uk*

1 With your back to the **Crown Inn**, follow the road to the left for 150 yards before taking a right turn down to the church. Go through the churchyard, passing to the left of the church, before veering right on a path down to the B4479. Follow this road to the right and in 100 yards, immediately past **Lower Brook House**, turn left along a side lane. Continue following what becomes a track ahead until it reaches a barn in 350 yards. At this point, the track bears left but for the walk keep ahead along a path that passes to the right of the barn before continuing along the right edge of a field to reach a gate. Follow an enclosed path to the next gate then continue across the hilltop to reach one final gate. Walk ahead for 35 yards before veering right across the field to a gate in the left-hand hedgerow and a road.

2 Turn left and, in 600 yards, right into **Batsford village**. In 200 yards, at a junction, turn sharply left and follow a tree-lined lane

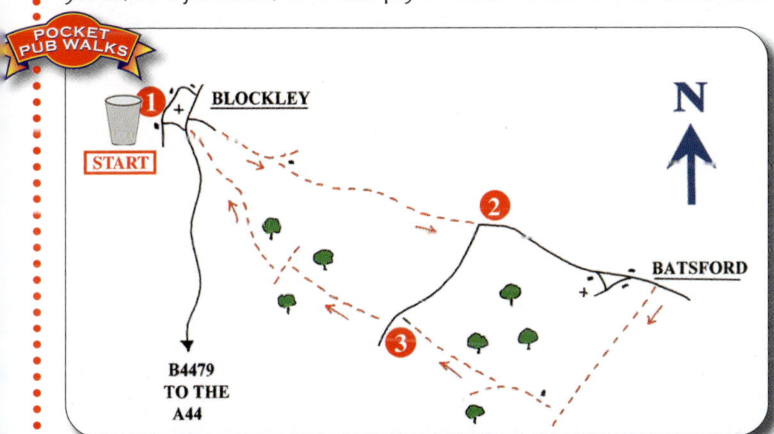

*The glorious woodland at Batsford*

back to the main road. Turn right and, in 75 yards, turn right at a handgate onto a footpath. Beyond an enclosed section of path, follow the path ahead across the right edges of five fields, with **Batsford Park** away to the right. On the far side of the fifth field, pass through a gate, turn right and follow the edge of the field ahead towards a cottage. Pass through a handgate to the left of this property, cross a drive to a handgate opposite and follow a field path ahead up to a stile and woodland. Follow a footpath into the woodland to a track and continue along this track for 200 yards to a point where it bears left. At this point, keep ahead on a path that reaches a gate and lane in 400 yards.

3 Follow the path opposite – initially a track – that then runs across the left edges of two fields to reach another track. Having enjoyed a fine view across **Blockley**, turn left and, in 100 yards, cross a stile on the right and walk down a hillside field to a gate in its bottom right corner. Drop downhill in the next field, crossing a farm access road, before passing a telegraph pole to reach a gate in the bottom field boundary. Beyond this gate, follow the right edge of the following field to the next gate before continuing along an enclosed path to reach the B4479. Turn left and, in 100 yards, turn right into **School Lane**. Follow this lane up to its junction with the **High Street** and turn left back to the **Crown Inn**.

## Place of interest nearby

**Batsford Arboretum** is a rare and beautiful collection of trees, shrubs and wild flowers located in 55 acres of spectacular Cotswold countryside. Visitors can wander along magical meandering paths beside streams and plants such as magnolias, candelabra primulas, and Japanese cherry blossom. In autumn, the trees explode into reds, deep purples, yellows and gold set against the bottle green of the evergreen foliage. Open all year round; visit www.batsarb.co.uk for details of times and other information.

# 2 Ford

## *The Plough Inn*

**Ford is a pleasant place** but, with its location on a busy road, few visitors come this way other than to sample the delights of the Plough Inn. Step aside from the main road, however, and there is an archetypal Cotswold landscape of gently rolling hills and sheep pasture, pretty villages and ancient churches. 'As lovely as any part of the Cotswolds is the valley of the Windrush where Temple Guiting lies', wrote Arthur Mee. The name is linked with the Knights Templars – the church was once given to the preceptor of Quenington, itself owned by that band of knights. Having passed Pinnock Farm, where the earthworks

**Distance** – 4 miles.

**OS Outdoor Leisure** 45 The Cotswolds. GR SP088294. An undulating, rather than hilly, landscape. There is one gentle climb out of Temple Guiting where the lane is labelled with a black arrow that represents a gradient of between 14% and 20%.

**Starting point** The Plough Inn at Ford.

***How to get there*** *Ford lies 7 miles west of Stow-on-the-Wold on the B4077 road. The Plough Inn is on the main road in the centre of the village and has a good-sized parking area for patrons.*

mark the site of the medieval village of Pinnock, and the Cotswold Hill Quarry where the golden local stone is extracted, the final port of call is Cutsdean. One story goes that there was an Anglo-Saxon chief called Cod and that the village was subsequently named 'Cod's dene'. There is even a theory that the hill country roundabout became known as 'Cod's wold', hence the Cotswolds.

THE PUB The **Plough Inn** has a rich history. Lovingly crafted from the local golden limestone in the 17th century, it saw service as a court house with the cellar being used as a lock up. An altogether warmer welcome awaits today's visitor, however, as is evident from a sign reading 'Ye weary travellers that pass by ... step in and quaff my nut brown ale ... twill make your lagging trotters dance'. Part of the Donnington Brewery estate based in nearby Moreton-in-Marsh, the Plough offers both the BB and SBA, two of the county's finest ales, brewed from water drawn from a spring alongside the brewery. The Plough's extensive garden is simply one of the best places to enjoy some rest and refreshment in this corner of the wolds.

*Open all day, every day in the summer months with food available all day. Opening hours are the usual lunchtimes and evenings in the winter months.*
☎ *01386 584215; postcode: GL54 5RU;*
*www.theploughinnatford.co.uk*

1 With your back to the pub, follow the B4077 to the right in the direction of **Stow**. In 250 yards, turn right onto a footpath and walk through an area of bushes to a stile. Follow the right edges

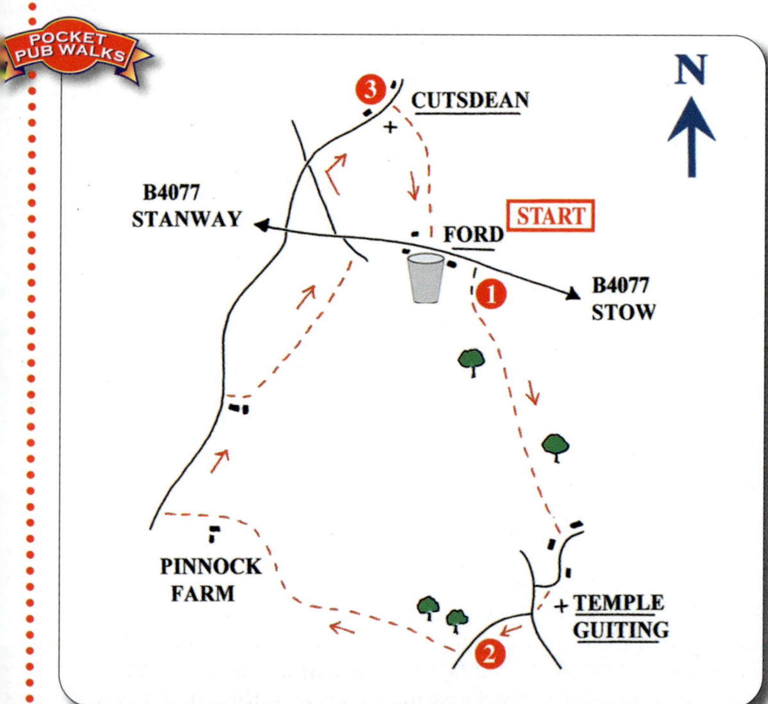

Temple Guiting's delightful church

of the next four fields to a gate before continuing along a track to a road by the manor in **Temple Guiting**. Follow this road to the right for 200 yards to a left turn leading to the church. Turn left and, in just one pace, right along an enclosed path that runs through to a road – detouring ahead to explore the church. Turn left at this road and, in 10 yards, right along a lane signposted as 'Unsuitable for motors'. In ¼ mile, at the top of a climb, pass through a copse before turning right along a public bridleway.

2 Follow this winding track across the hilltop, passing through gates along the way, until in ¾ mile it reaches a lane. Follow the path opposite for ¼ mile to a road. Turn right and, in ½ mile, just past **Slade Barn**, turn right onto a public footpath. Follow this enclosed path for ¼ mile and, just beyond a quarry, follow the right edge

of a field down to a road. Turn left to a junction, cross the B4077 and follow the road opposite for 400 yards to a junction. Follow the road to the right for another 400 yards into **Cutsdean**.

3 Just past the entrance to **Cutsdean Farm**, turn right along a footpath to a stile. Follow the right edge of the field ahead, with the village church on the right, to a stile on the right in 200 yards. Cross this stile and walk ahead across the next field. Towards the far side of the field, veer left to a stile in the left-hand field boundary. Keep ahead on a path that bears right through woodland to a junction of paths. Turn left and follow an enclosed path between horse paddocks to reach a metalled track. Turn right and follow this track down to a gate and the B4077. Turn left back to the **Plough**.

## Place of interest nearby

**Stow-on-the-Wold**, standing 700 feet above sea-level at a point where eight roads converge, has a wealth of interest for the visitor. There is the Square with its weekly market, where Charter Fairs have also been held since 1107 when Henry I granted borough status to what was then called 'Edwardstow'. The name possibly came from Edward the Hermit, a shadowy figure from early Christian times. Edward also lent his name to St Edward's House, St Edward's Hall and St Edward's church with its medieval origins. Stow can also boast a good number of antique and gift shops, making it quite the perfect place for visitors who like to browse for a possible bargain. The website www.stowonthewold.net gives further information on Stow-on-the-Wold.

# 3 Guiting Power

## *The Farmers Arms*

**Guiting Power and Naunton**, the two villages that feature on this delightful walk, lie alongside the upper reaches of the River Windrush. Guiting Power, where the charming stone cottages and houses lie clustered around a small green, is a picturesque spot that shows the art of the Cotswold stonemasons at their very best. Naunton is, if it could be possible, even more attractive. Essentially one long street of Cotswold cottages and country gardens, its setting in a wooded valley would be hard to better. Certain to catch the eye are the church with its handsome Perpendicular tower with pinnacles and gargoyles, as well as a dovecote that dates from 1600 when doves were valued as meat. It has a staggering 1,176 nest holes.

**Distance** – 5 miles.

**OS Outdoor Leisure** 45 The Cotswolds. GR SP096248. Some gentle climbs in and around the Upper Windrush Valley, with the most demanding climb being a relatively moderate 200 ft ascent out of Naunton.

**Starting point** The Farmers Arms in Guiting Power.

***How to get there*** *Taking the B4068, turn off 7 miles west of Stow-on-the-Wold and follow an unclassified road into Guiting Power. The pub lies just below the green in the centre of the village, where there is ample room for considerate roadside parking.*

THE PUB

The **Farmers Arms** presents a most handsome exterior to the visitor. The golden stone walls, traditional stone stiles and colourful hanging baskets are matched by a charming interior where we find stripped stonework and old flagstones. As well as fine real ales from the Donnington Brewery based near Moreton-in-Marsh, the Farmers Arms offers what has been described as 'unpretentious food' from sandwiches upwards. It is certainly one of very few pubs where I have seen fishfinger sandwiches on the menu, a real throw back for somebody of my generation. With so many pubs in the Cotswolds moving upmarket, it was a treat to find such a down-to-earth and traditional hostelry as this.

*Open lunchtimes and evenings, with food served from 12 noon to 2 pm and 6.30 pm to 9 pm.*
☎ *01451 850358; postcode: GL54 5TZ*

1 With your back to the **Farmers Arms**, follow the road to the right. Take a left turn off the green towards the church and, where this

road bears right, keep ahead along a cul de sac to the church. Pass through handgates by the church into a field. Follow the left edge of this field to a gate before heading across the next field, bearing slightly left all the while, to reach a gate. Drop downhill in the next field, cross a stream – with a dam and lake to the right – before following a stepped path uphill to a gate at the top of the field ahead. Walk the length of the next field to reach a gate and

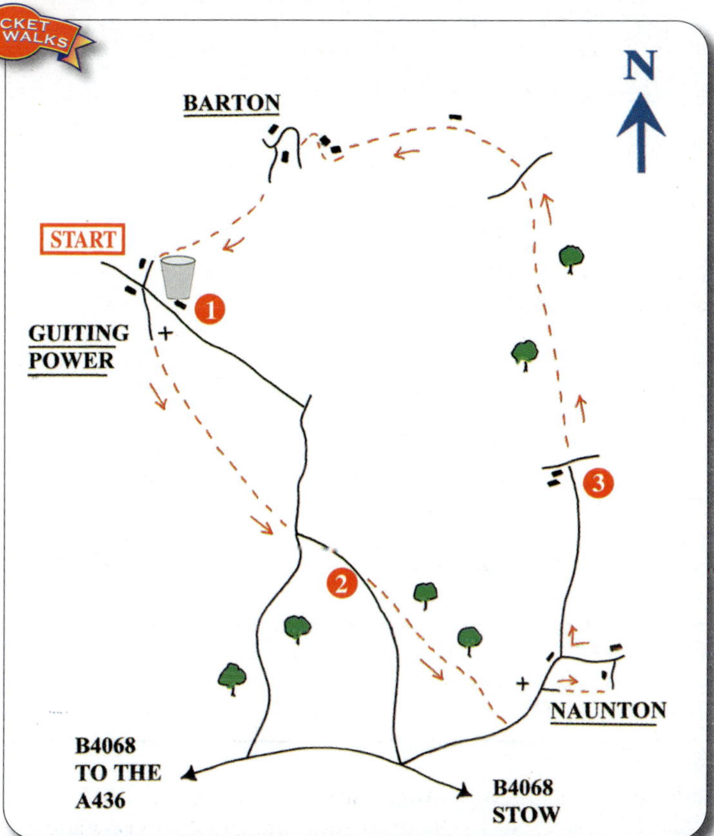

*Naunton, seen from the route*

road junction, before following the road ahead signposted to **Naunton** and **Stow**.

2 In 200 yards, pass through a gateway on the left and turn right to follow a track along the right edge of a field. Enter a second field and walk ahead, bearing slightly left all the while. Almost in the corner of the field, pass through a gate on the left before walking across the corner of the following field to reach a gate and lane. Follow this lane to the left down into **Naunton** and, after 300 yards, turn right along a no through road. In 200 yards, beyond a gate and stile, veer left at a fork and follow a path through a valley bottom to another gate. Follow the path beyond this gate, with the **Windrush** on the left, to a stile and lane. Turn left up to the main road in Naunton before turning left. In 350 yards, just past a Baptist chapel, the road bears left at a junction. At this point, keep ahead along a side road that bears right to climb out of Naunton and reach a junction by **Grange Hill Farm** in ½ mile.

3 Follow the track opposite for ¾ mile to its junction with a road, passing quarries along the way. Turn right and, in 200 yards, left

along a track. Follow this track for 1 mile to its junction with a lane in the hamlet of **Barton**. Turn right, cross the infant Windrush and then take a left turn along a side lane signposted as being 'Unsuitable for motor vehicles'. In 150 yards, where the lane bears right, keep ahead along a driveway marked as a footpath – it leads to **Little Windrush Farm**. Pass to the right of the farm to a stile before following the left edges of the next two fields. In the following field, bear half-right across to a stile in its far right corner. Follow a footpath to the left downhill to a footbridge over a stream and a gate. Continue along a path to another gate before continuing along a back lane to its junction with the main road in **Guiting Power**, where you will find the **Farmers Arms** to the left.

## Place of interest nearby

**Sudeley Castle** near Winchombe lies just 5 miles from Guiting Power. Set against the beautiful backdrop of the wolds, it is regarded as one of England's most romantic castles. It has royal connections spanning a thousand years and has played an important role in the turbulent and changing times of England's past. Sudeley was once the magnificent palace of Queen Katherine Parr, Henry VIII's last and surviving wife, who is buried in the Castle church. Henry VIII, Anne Boleyn, Lady Jane Grey and Elizabeth I all stayed at Sudeley Castle. Charles I resided here while his nephew Prince Rupert established Sudeley as his garrison headquarters during the English Civil War. Surrounding the castle are ten magnificent gardens, each with their own special beauty and charm. Centrepiece is the Queen's Garden, named after Katherine Parr and famous for its magnificent collection of old-fashioned roses interspersed with fragrant herbs and surrounded by yew hedges and fine examples of topiary. Visit www.sudeleycastle.co.uk for further information.

POCKET PUB WALKS

# 4 Bourton-on-the-Water

## *The Kingsbridge Inn*

**No walking tour** of the Cotswolds would be complete without a visit to Bourton-on-the-Water – the 'Venice of the Cotswolds' – and the Slaughters. Even on the busiest of days, Bourton's crowds are soon left behind as the walk crosses undulating countryside to reach Lower and Upper Slaughter. In Lower Slaughter, the cottages sit overlooking Slaughter Brook, whose waters power a brick-built corn mill, now a popular tourist attraction. A few fields away lies Upper Slaughter, with its Norman church, Elizabethan manor and picture-postcard cottages centred upon a small green. Bridlepaths and lanes climb the hillsides to the south of the Slaughters to return to the Windrush Valley, with the river being followed back into Bourton-on-the-Water.

**Distance** – 5 miles.

**OS Outdoor Leisure** 45 The Cotswolds. GR SP168210. Well-defined paths that cross a moderately undulating landscape.

**Starting point** The public pay & display car park in Bourton-on-the-Water. There is only short-term roadside parking in the village.

***How to get there*** *Bourton-on-the-Water lies 4 miles south of Stow-on-the-Wold on the A429 Cirencester road. The car park is behind a garage as you enter Bourton.*

THE PUB The **Kingsbridge Inn** enjoys one of the best locations in the Cotswolds. This handsome stone building sits on the green in the centre of Bourton-on-the-Water literally overlooking the River Windrush. If you are fortunate enough to find one of the outside tables vacant, this is quite the perfect place to simply sit and watch the world go by. The menu extends from sandwiches upwards and includes fresh salads and fish dishes, grills and light bites, as well as main dishes that could include options such as lamb shoulder or steak and ale pie. With beers that include Marston's Pedigree and Banks's Bitter, staples from the Midlands, the Kingsbridge will prove a real delight at the end of a fine walk in the wolds.

*The Kingsbridge Inn is open all day and serves throughout opening hours.*

☎ *01451 824119; postcode: GL54 2BS; www.kingsbridgepub.co.uk*

1 Walk down to the bottom of the car park and follow a tarmac path signposted to 'The Village'. At the first junction turn right

and follow a path along to a road. Continue following the path opposite past some cottages and on to a church on the left and a school on the right. Carry on along the path beyond the school for 200 yards until its bears right to cross an old railway. Beyond the trackbed, follow the right edge of a field over to the A429. Cross the main road to a pair of stiles in the hedge opposite before walking over the next field to another stile. Cross the following

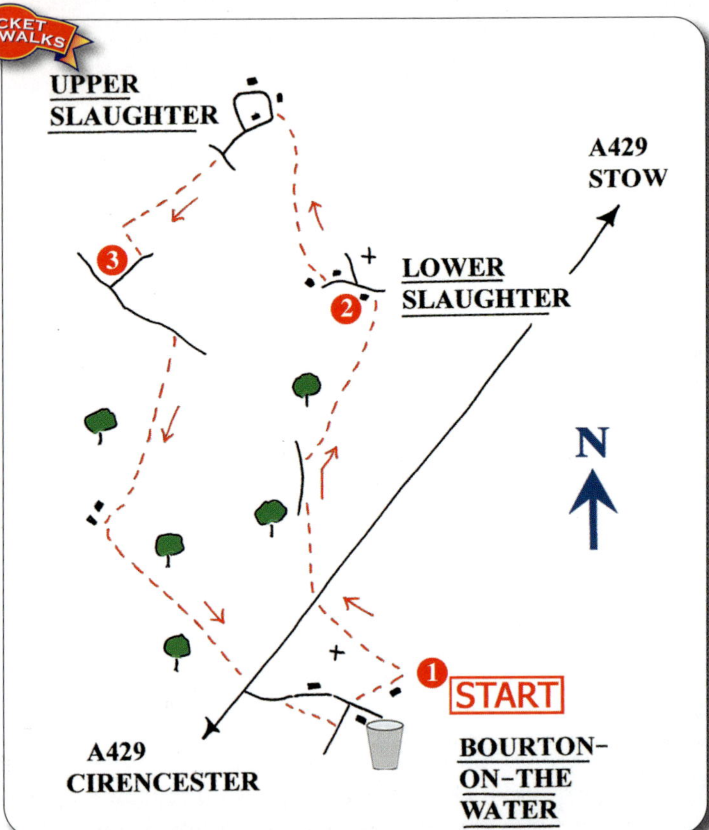

*Upper Slaughter*

field, bearing slightly right all the while, to reach a lane. Turn right and, in 250 yards, pass through a gate on the right and follow an enclosed path for 300 yards down to a junction. Turn left and follow what is a tarmac path through to the road in **Lower Slaughter**.

2 Turn left and, at a junction by the church, turn left along the road to the **Mill Museum** and **Upper Slaughter**. In a few paces, turn right onto a cul de sac road signposted as 'Access Only'. Keep on this road and, immediately past the **Old Mill**, turn left along a tarmac path to a gate. Continue along the path to a gate before crossing a field to a gate in the hedgerow opposite. Walk the whole length of the next field to a gate before continuing along a path that drops gradually downhill to another gate. Keep ahead to the road in **Upper Slaughter**. Turn right and, after 100 yards, turn left along a road leading to a 'Deep Ford'. At the ford, cross a bridge on the left and follow a road to a junction just past **The Square**. Turn right to reach a junction in 100 yards. Pass through a gateway opposite and follow a footpath up the right edge of a field. At the top of the field, pass through a gate on the right into

a paddock. Turn left and, in a few paces, pass through a gate on the left. Follow a path for 200 yards to a road, turn right and walk uphill to a road junction.

3 Turn left – signposted to Bourton – and in 250 yards fork right along a track. Beyond a gate, follow the path across the left edges of two fields before continuing along an enclosed course. At a junction by a stable and garden, turn left along the **Windrush Way**. Follow an enclosed path to a gate, before following the right edge of a field to a gate and enclosed path leading down to the A429. Cross the A429 and follow the road opposite into **Bourton**, bordering the Windrush. In 200 yards, with **Mill Cottage** on the left, turn right along a path waymarked the 'Windrush Way'. On reaching the river, cross a bridge and follow the Windrush downstream. In 200 yards, keep on the path as it veers right away from the river to a handgate before following a path down to a back lane in Bourton. Turn left up to the Windrush, turn right and walk along to **High Bridge**. Cross the river and the **High Street** (to visit the **Kingsbridge Inn**, follow the **High Street** to the right for 100 yards to reach the pub) before following a paved path opposite to the right of the **Dial House Hotel**. In 100 yards, at a junction, turn left for a few paces and then right back to the car park.

## Places of interest nearby

Bourton-on-the-Water has many attractions. In addition to the **Old New Inn's Model Village** (☎ 01451 820467), visitors can enjoy **Birdland**, a park and gardens that contain over 500 birds (☎ 01451 820480). There is also the **Cotswold Motor Museum and Toy Collection** (☎ 01451 821255) and the **Cotswold Perfumery Limited** (☎ 01451 820698). The website www.bourtoninfo.com gives details of all of these attractions and more besides.

# 5 Swinbrook

## *The Swan Inn*

**Arthur Mee's guidebook** to Gloucestershire was rather perfunctory concerning the River Windrush. In this volume of *The King's England*, Mee noted that 'the Windrush comes south from near Temple Guiting and, after collecting the waters of the Dickler and making Bourton-on-the-Water a miniature Venice with its bridges, enters Oxfordshire'. It deserves so much more than that. Downstream of Burford, the water meadows are an absolute delight, especially when sheep and new-born lambs are grazing in the riverside pastures. With swans, moorhens, coots and ducks making their home along the riverbank, it is a quintessentially English scene. There are also the villages along

**Distance** – 4 miles.

**OS Outdoor Leisure** 45 The Cotswolds. GR SP283119. Field paths and quiet lanes on a generally flat terrain.

**Starting point** The Swan Inn at Swinbrook.

***How to get there*** *Swinbrook is reached on an unclassified road 2 miles east of Burford, off the A40. The Swan is on the left as you enter the village. As well as its own car park, there are places for roadside parking in the vicinity of the inn.*

the way: Swinbrook itself, Widford and Asthall, with stone churches, cottages and mills to catch the eye. St Oswald's church in Widford is a gem. Standing in splendid isolation in the middle of meadowland due to the medieval village alongside being abandoned at the time of the Black Death, the interior with its box pews and wall paintings is wonderfully unspoilt.

**THE PUB**

'We plunged into a world that felt as startlingly remote as if we'd dropped down Alice in Wonderland's rabbit-hole and popped out in paradise,' wrote one reviewer of the **Swan**. This stone-built, 400-year-old pub, with its splendid wisteria climbing all over the front walls, really is an unspoilt village inn. With its flagstone flooring, beams, simple antique furnishings and wood-burning stove, it exudes a most traditional atmosphere. The food is exemplary, as is the choice of fine local beers. These might typically include brews from the Cotswold Brewing Company, as well as Hook Norton Best from just down the road.

*Opening hours are 11 am to 3 pm and 6 pm to 11.30 pm.*
*☎ 01993 823339; postcode: OX18 4DY;*
*www.theswanswinbrook.co.uk*

1 With your back to the **Swan**, follow the road to the left. Ignoring the first right turn, continue to the next junction by a small green in the centre of the village. Just past this junction, follow a footpath on the left that runs between a pair of cottages and past the church. Beyond a gate, continue along the enclosed path to a gate and open field. Walk ahead across this field to a gate and stile opposite before crossing a second field to a gate just below **Widford's church**. Continue following a track across a field to a gate and lane in **Widford**. Turn left, cross the **Windrush** and, at the next junction, follow the road to the left for ½ mile to a crossroads. Follow the lane opposite, signposted to **Asthall** and continue for ½ mile.

2 Just before an avenue of beech trees, turn left along a road into the centre of **Asthall**. Keep on this road as it bears right to reach a junction just past the **Maytime Inn**. Turn left and, in 150 yards, right along a cul de sac lane towards **Asthall Farm**. Keep on what is a bridlepath as it bears right in front of the farmhouse, and stay on the track for 300 yards as it runs along the right edge of a field. On the far side of the field, turn left – there is a marker post – and



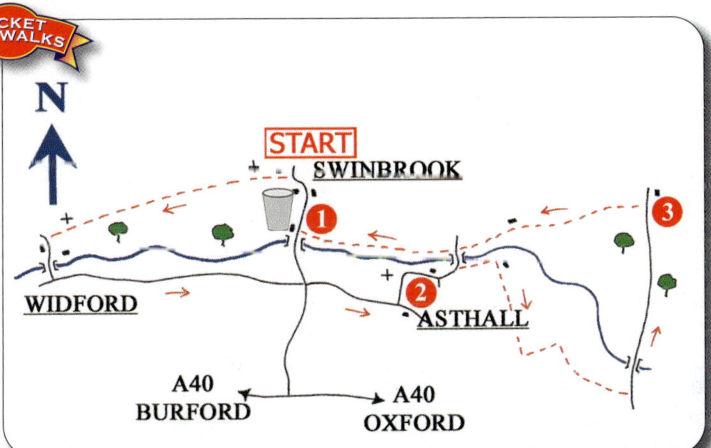

*The tranquil River Windrush*

follow the track as it runs down the end field boundary. At the bottom of the field, turn right and follow the bridleway across three fields to join a lane. Follow the lane to the left across the Windrush before continuing for just over ½ mile to a property on the right called **Stonefold**.

3 At this point, pass through a gateway on the left and follow a footpath ahead, keeping a field boundary on the right-hand side. Beyond a gate in the corner of the field, follow the right edge of the next field until the field boundary ends. Continue walking ahead, passing to the left of **Kitesbridge Farm**, before following the Windrush upstream over two fields to join a lane by a bridge. Cross to a stile opposite and follow a well-worn path over the field ahead to a stile in the end field boundary, the Windrush meandering away to the left. Beyond this stile, head across to a gateway in the far right-hand corner of the following field. Walk diagonally across the next field to its far left corner, making for a stile just past a cottage on the left. Join the lane and turn left back to the **Swan Inn**.

*On the route back to Swinbrook*

## Places of interest nearby

**Burford**, just a couple of miles from Swinbrook, is often described as the 'gateway to the Cotswolds' by visitors from the south-east of England. The High Street slopes down from the high wolds, with their beautiful views over the open countryside, to the willow-fringed River Windrush where a fine three-arched medieval bridge crosses the river at the foot of the hill. Sure to catch the eye is St John the Baptist church, with its almost cathedral-like proportions. It was built from around 1175 and is described in Simon Jenkins' book *England's Thousand Best Churches* as the 'Queen of Oxfordshire, a paragon and museum of the English Parish Church'. Visit www.burfordcotswolds.co.uk for more information on the town.

POCKET PUB WALKS

# 6 Chedworth

## *The Seven Tuns*

**Chedworth is an attractive Cotswold village**, whose traditional stone cottages and houses hug the steep sides of a tributary valley of the Coln. St Andrew's church, with its sculpture of the Madonna and Child by Helen Frazer Rock, sits alongside the 17th-century manor and its grounds on Queen Street, so-named following a visit from Queen Elizabeth of York in 1491. In the neighbouring valley lies Chedworth Roman Villa, with its fine mosaics and bathhouses, hypocausts and water shrine, as well as a recently constructed museum that provides visitors

**Distance** – 4½ miles.

**OS Outdoor Leisure** 45 The Cotswolds. GR SP053120. Steep hillsides, valleys and shady woodland.

**Starting point** Chedworth church, immediately above the Seven Tuns inn.

***How to get there*** *Follow the A429 north from Cirencester for 7 miles before taking a left turn signposted to Chedworth village – not the Roman villa – just ½ mile beyond Foss Cross and the Hare and Hounds. Follow this unclassified road for 2 miles to a sharp right turn signposted to Chedworth and Yanworth. As you enter Chedworth, turn left along a cul-de-sac lane just above the Seven Tuns where you will find a parking area outside the church.*

with a fascinating insight into the way of life in this remote valley all those years ago. Deep in Chedworth Woods, just above the villa, lie the remains of the long disused railway that ran from Cheltenham through the Cotswolds towards the South Coast. A mile of the former trackbed now forms the Chedworth Nature Reserve, where exposed Cotswold limestone, lime-rich springs and ancient beech woodland provide habitats for a rich array of flora and fauna that includes bats and deer, dormice and lizards … even Roman snails whose ancestors were imported by the ancient Romans!

THE PUB The name 'tuns' refers to brewers' fermenting vats and, with springs of water bubbling out of the ground opposite the **Seven Tuns**, there is no doubt that this hostelry was once based around a small brewery. This attractive 17th-century stone inn, with its traditional bars, is wonderfully atmospheric, whilst nothing could be more tranquil than sitting outside the pub on a warm summer's day watching water cascading from one of the local springs. A range of Young's beers is available at the Seven Tuns, including their Bitter, Special and Seasonal ales, as well as a regular guest beer. There is also an excellent range of home-made food, although this is not available on a Sunday evening.

*Opening times on Monday to Saturday are 12 noon to 3 pm and 6 pm to 11pm; Sunday 12 noon to 3 pm and 7 pm to 10.30 pm.*
☎ *01285 720242; postcode: GL54 4AE*

1 With your back to the church, follow the lane to the left until it ends at a stile, ignoring a right fork along the way. Turn left and walk the whole length of a field to a stile in the end field boundary

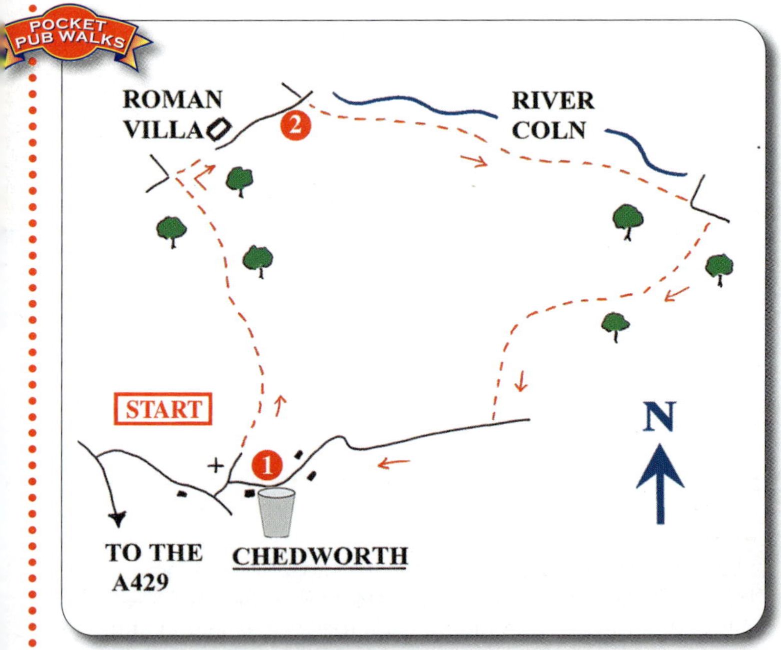

*Chedworth Roman Villa*

just below a belt of trees. Follow a stepped path up through the tree cover to a stile before walking along a short section of enclosed path to a handgate. Continue along the right edge of the field ahead to reach a gate leading into **Chedworth Woods**. Follow the woodland path for 400 yards to a junction, turn right and take a waymarked path to **Chedworth Roman Villa**. Follow the road down past the villa for 250 yards to a crossroads.

2 Turn right and follow a private road – footpath only – for just over 1 mile to its junction with another road. Follow the road ahead for 20 yards before turning right onto a footpath that runs through

**Chedworth Woods**. On reaching a prominent track, keep ahead for 20 yards before veering left to drop downhill into a shallow valley. Follow the path through the valley bottom until it reaches the end of the woodland. Continue along a path that bears left uphill in a field to a marker post before continuing ahead across the field to a junction by a tree. Carry on across the open field to a gate and lane. Follow the lane to the right for 600 yards until it drops downhill into **Chedworth**. Continue following the road through the village back to the **Seven Tuns**.

## Places of interest nearby

**Northleach**, just a few miles north-east of Chedworth along the A429, is a delightful Cotswold town centred around a market place with half-timbered buildings and merchants' houses dating from the 16th century. At the crossroads at the entrance to the town stands the '**House of Correction**', dating from the era of severe sharp punishments! Reminders of the great days of the wool trade are everywhere in the town, most evidently the impressive **church of St Peter and St Paul**, a fine example of the Cotswold Perpendicular style. One of the most fascinating attractions in Northleach is Keith Harding's '**World of Mechanical Music**'. This museum occupies the Oak House, once home to a wealthy wool merchant. The museum contains a collection of instruments in the old school room, including barrel pianos, musical boxes, polyphons and automata. The museum also offers a world-renowned workshop. The website www.northleach.gov.uk gives further information.

POCKET PUB WALKS

# 7 Quenington

## *The Keepers Arms*

**Quenington has been described as** 'a highly attractive village with many pleasant houses and cottages on slopes above the little River Coln'. The church is wonderful, especially the tympanum over the south and north doorways. The former depicts the Coronation of the Virgin, with the latter displaying the Harrowing of Hell. These Norman doorways are clearly amongst the finest in all Gloucestershire and represent outstanding examples of Romanesque art. Neighbouring Coln St Aldwyns is an equally delightful village, with its church and Elizabethan manor house enjoying a slightly elevated location above the River Coln and an area of beech woodland beyond. The riverside paths alongside the Coln are always appealing. This is the English landscape at its very best, with traditional waterside

**Distance** – 5½ miles.

**OS Outdoor Leisure** 45 The Cotswolds. GR SP146042. Field paths, tracks and lanes that cross a gently undulating landscape.

**Starting point** The Keepers Arms in Quenington.

***How to get there*** *Leave the A417 in Fairford and follow an unclassified road in a northerly direction signposted to Quenington and Coln St Aldwyns. In 2 miles, a right turn leads into the centre of Quenington, where the Keepers Arms lies on the left-hand side of the main street. As well as the pub car park, there is also ample roadside parking.*

meadows, sheep and cattle grazing in a timeless fashion, a rich array of wildfowl and much prized trout easy to spot in the Coln's clear waters.

THE PUB

The **Keepers Arms** is an attractive Cotswold stone building, with exposed stonework, low beams and open fireplaces, everything a visitor would expect from a pub in this neck of the woods. This is one of those places that has managed to strike the right balance between offering excellent cuisine whilst not pricing out locals who just want to put the world to rights whilst enjoying a quiet pint. Alongside the wide variety of food, the selection of real ales is what will certainly catch the eye. The brews could typically include West Country beers from Stroud and Butcombe in Somerset, as well as Timothy Taylor's from Yorkshire.

*Open usual pub hours, with food served from Wednesday to Sunday at lunchtimes only.*

☎ *01285 750349; postcode: GL7 5BL; www.thekeepersarms.co.uk*

1 With your back to the **Keepers Arms**, follow the road to the left downhill to reach a junction, with a side road going off on the left. At this point, turn right along a drive and, where this driveway bears left to a barn, keep ahead along a grassy path. Continue to

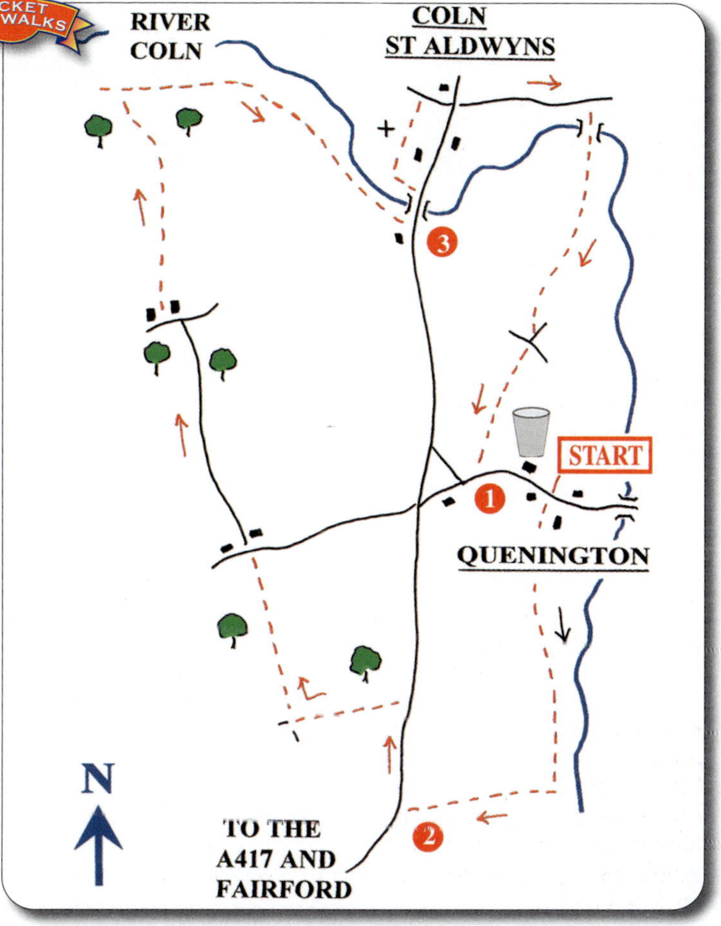

*Cattle grazing along the way*

a gateway, before heading across the right edge of the next field. On the far side of the field, continue following a path bordering the **River Coln** on the left. Where this path bears right up into a field, continue ahead along a path bordering the Coln; this bears right in 350 yards up into a field. Turn left and follow the left edge of this field around to a gateway in its corner before following the left edge of the next field to a gate and lane.

2 Turn right and, in 350 yards, at the end of a wall, left along a track that follows the right edge of a field, with a wind pump in the field on the left. Follow this track to the corner of the field and, in the next field, turn immediately right to take a track down to a road by **Donkeywell Farm**. Follow the track opposite for ¾ mile until it reaches a road just past **Coneygar Wood**. Turn left and, in 200 yards, turn right onto a track that runs between two properties. Follow this track for 400 yards down to **Ash Copse** on the left. Just inside this copse, turn left onto an obvious path that runs through the middle of the woodland to reach a gate and hillside field. Turn right and, at the bottom of the field, right along a field path just before the **Coln** to a gate. Continue along an enclosed path to a gate and meadow. Walk across this meadow,

with the Coln on the left, to a gate on the far side of the field. Follow the left edge of the next field and, in 200 yards, veer left into the adjoining field. Follow the right edge of this field along the next field before following its right edge, with woodland on the right. At the end of the field, continue ahead through the woodland into the next field. Follow the path across this field to a gate and lodge on the edge of **Coln St Aldwyns**.

3 Join a road, turn left across the **Coln** and then immediately left along a drive that leads along to **Upper Mill**. Just before the entrance to this property, cross a footbridge on the right and follow a path up to a back lane in Coln St Aldwyns. Follow this lane ahead to a junction and turn right down to a junction by the village shop. Follow the road ahead towards Hatherop and Lechlade. In ¼ mile, just as the walk enters **Hatherop**, cross a bridge on the right over the River Coln. Keep ahead to a gate before walking directly ahead across three fields, passing through gateways along the way, to reach a lane on the edge of Quenington. Turn right to a junction, and follow the green lane ahead – a footpath – through to a green and junction in the centre of **Quenington**. Turn left to return to the **Keepers Arms**.

## Places of interest nearby

**Bibury** lies just a short drive north-west of Quenington. Once described as 'the most beautiful village in the Cotswolds', this really is an enchanting place. The attractions in the village include the much photographed **Arlington Row** – a rank of delightful weavers' cottages – the **Bibury Trout Farm**, **Arlington Mill** and the outstanding **St Mary's church**. The whole setting is made all the more perfect by the sparkling waters of the Coln, where spotting the local trout appears to be a popular pastime. Visit www.bibury.com for more information on Bibury.

POCKET PUB WALKS

# 8 Miserden

## *The Carpenters Arms*

**Finding Miserden is** half the battle on this walk. It lies along a network of quiet lanes above the Upper Frome Valley, and is certainly far from the madding crowd. Both villages on the walk – Miserden and Edgeworth – have much to interest the visitor. Miserden church has been much restored but does boast an elaborately-carved and gilded reredos, as well as a fine series of 17th-century monuments. The war memorial opposite the church is the work of Sir Edwyn Lutyens, who also worked on the Elizabethan mansion in nearby Misarden Park. There could be few more perfect groupings than that of the church and manor in Edgeworth. Again, the church has been the subject of much restoration, but some of the glass and the churchyard cross date from medieval times. The manor was originally Jacobean but was restored and enlarged in the 19th century. Between the villages

**Distance** – 6½ miles.

**OS Explorer** 179 Cheltenham, Gloucester & Stroud. GR SO938089.
Hillsides and valley bottoms, with a few steep ascents and descents along the way.

**Starting point** The Carpenters Arms in Miserden.

***How to get there*** *From the A419 between Cirencester and Stroud, take the turn off northwards to Sapperton, 3 miles from Cirencester. In Sapperton, follow the signs downhill to the Daneway Inn. Immediately past the inn, turn right and follow a lane waymarked to Miserden. In 3½ miles, a right turn leads into the village where there is room for roadside parking by the Carpenters Arms.*

lies an archetypal stretch of the Frome Valley, with steep wooded hillsides, sheltered valley bottoms and handsome stone properties. An altogether fine walk in a little-explored part of the wolds.

The **Carpenters Arms** is just what you would expect of a traditional Cotswold pub. The bars have low beams, old wooden tables on bare boards, exposed stonework and welcoming open fires in the winter. Summer visitors can enjoy watching the world go by from the picnic tables at the front of this fine old stone inn. The menu offers a varied and mouth-watering array of starters, including breaded prawns and creamy garlic mushrooms, to be followed by main courses that could include home-made steak and Guinness pie, local sausage and mash and home-baked ham. Finally, if you've room, do sample one of the delicious home-made puddings. The Carpenters Arms delivers everything you'd expect from a country pub and more.

*Open Monday to Thursday from 11.30 am to 3 pm and 6.30 pm to 11 pm; Friday and Saturday 11.30 am to 3 pm and 6 pm to 12 midnight; Sunday 12 noon to 4 pm and 7 pm to 10.30 pm.*
*☎ 0845 200 9275; postcode: GL6 7JA*

1 Facing the pub, follow the road to the left out of the village back up to the junction with the road that came up from the **Daneway Inn**. Turn left towards **Cirencester** and, in 20 yards, turn right along a signposted footpath by **Lypiatt Cottage**. Beyond an enclosed section of path, follow the left edge of a field to a gate and back lane. Follow this lane to the left for 200 yards to a junction. Cross the road ahead and follow a footpath opposite to the right of a post box. On reaching a stile, follow the right edge of a field to a gap in the iron fence ahead. Cross a track, pass through a gap in the fence opposite and turn right to a stile in the corner of the field. Cross the following field to a stone slab stile on the right and enter **Fox Wood**. Follow the main woodland path ahead and, at the first junction, turn left. At the next junction, a T-junction, keep left once again and keep on the track until it emerges in an open field. Follow a track across the right edge of this open field. On the far side of the field, where this track bears right, continue following the right edge of the next field to a gate and road.

2 Turn right and, in a few paces, take the left turn to **Edgeworth**. In 300 yards, keep left at a junction by some gates and, in 20 yards, turn right down a cul de sac waymarked to the church. In 250 yards, just past **School House** on the left, cross a stile on the left. Cross a field to a gate and follow an enclosed path up to **Edgeworth church**. Walk around to a road at the front of the church, turn left down to the entrance to **Edgeworth Manor** and, just before the entrance gates, follow a track on the right. Keep on this track as it drops downhill to cross the **River Frome** in the valley bottom, before continuing along the track as it climbs uphill to reach a junction with a lane in 250 yards. Turn left, drop

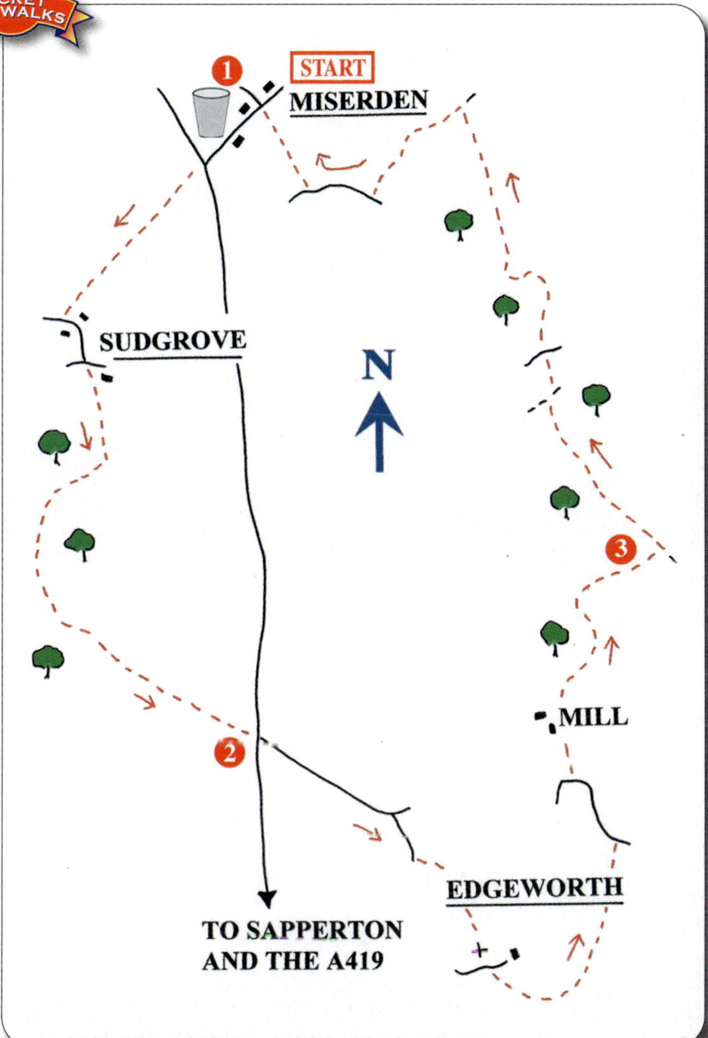
START
MISERDEN
1
SUDGROVE
N
2
3
MILL
EDGEWORTH
TO SAPPERTON
AND THE A419

*The lake at Misarden Park*

downhill into the valley bottom, cross the Frome once again and turn right in 50 yards along the gated drive leading up to **Edgeworth Mill Farm**. Having passed a pond on the right, veer right along a track that passes to the right of the property. Having crossed a footbridge, continue uphill for 50 yards before turning left to follow a path that passes above the property, with a fence on the left. In 200 yards, at a marker post just inside some woodland, turn right and follow a side path that climbs uphill to reach a track in 200 yards. Follow this track to the right uphill to a gate at the exit from the woodland.

3 Continue on the track ahead along the right edge of a hilltop field and, in the corner of the field, turn left to follow the end field boundary, keeping the boundary on the right. On the far side of

the field, continue following the track as it borders coniferous woodland on the left. At a fork, keep ahead, ignoring a path on the left dropping downhill. Keep following the track, ignoring the next left turn by a telegraph pole, and in 20 yards keep left at a fork and continue along the track to reach a lane. Cross a stile opposite uphill to a bump in the ground before bearing half-left to a stile at the entrance to some woodland. Follow a steep and occasionally stepped path up to the top of the woodland. Enter the field ahead and turn left to follow its left-hand boundary to the corner of the field. Enter the woodland ahead and follow a path to the right. In 300 yards, where a path goes off on the right to enter a field, keep left and follow a path that winds its way around the top of the woodland to reach a junction of paths in 350 yards, with a tarmac drive on the right. At this point, follow the track that drops downhill on the left to reach **Misarden Park Lake**. At a junction just past the lake, turn left and follow an estate road uphill before taking a right turn in 100 yards. At the next junction, ignore a track on the left, keeping ahead instead to a gate and field. Walk ahead uphill across this field to reach a gate and lane. Turn right and, in 250 yards, right along an enclosed path that leads back to the centre of **Miserden**, where a left turn will return you to the **Carpenters Arms**.

## Places of interest nearby

**Cirencester**, a busy market town, stands on the site of Corinium Dobunnorum. This was at one time Roman Britain's second largest city, and the meeting point of no fewer than three major Roman roads – the Ermin Way, the Fosse Way and Akeman Street. This makes a visit to the **Corinium Museum** and the well-preserved amphitheatre almost obligatory. Visit www.cirencester.co.uk for more information on the town and its attractions.

POCKET PUB WALKS

# 9 Slad

## *The Woolpack*

**The village of Slad** will for ever be associated with Laurie Lee, and *Cider with Rosie* in particular. Written in 1959, this is an account of growing up in that seemingly oh so innocent period after the First World War. It depicts a time of real community spirit, before the appearance of the motorcar and bike, an era that appears late on in the book in the chapter entitled 'Last Days'. Here he writes of how the arrival of the bus meant that towns were nearer, where 'pleasures were more anonymous and tasty'. The Cotswold landscape so vividly portrayed in this pastoral classic, however, has changed but little in the days since Laurie Lee penned what is the most famous account of life in the wolds. The cottages may be a little smarter but the steep hillsides and ancient woodland, the sparkling

**Distance** – 5½ miles.

**OS Explorer** 179 Gloucester, Cheltenham & Stroud. GR SO872073.
Well-defined tracks and paths in and around a Cotswold valley. Steep hillsides.

**Starting point** The Woolpack inn at Slad.

***How to get there*** *Leave the A46 at Stroud before following the B4070 to Slad. Park on the roadside in the vicinity of the Woolpack.*

streams and sheep pasture would be readily identifiable to anybody from that now far-off age.

THE PUB

The **Woolpack** is a marvellously unpretentious pub, probably little changed in decades. Old-fashioned tables and chairs, an open log fire in winter and the inevitable, but tasteful, shrine to Laurie Lee make this one of my favourite pubs in the region. Sitting on the edge of the hillside, the Woolpack also commands extensive views across the Slad Valley. The food is pretty decent, too, ranging from good-quality sandwiches and baguettes right through to generous hot meals using local produce wherever possible. Real ales from the nearby Uley Brewery – Old Spot is almost obligatory – together with local ciders also add to the appeal of the Woolpack.

*Open from 12 noon to 3 pm and from 6 pm to 11 pm, with food served from 12 noon to 2 pm and 7 pm to 9 pm except for Sunday evenings.*
☎ *01452 813429; postcode: G16 7QA;*
*www.the woolpackinn-slad.com*

1 With your back to the **Woolpack**, follow the B4070 to the left for 350 yards before turning right on a tarmac path – there is no marker post. Follow this path – it becomes a track – up to a hillside field. Follow the right edge of this field on uphill for 100 yards to a stile before continuing along a woodland path to reach a stile and lane on the hilltop. Turn right and follow this lane – it becomes a track – for 500 yards to a junction. Take the path

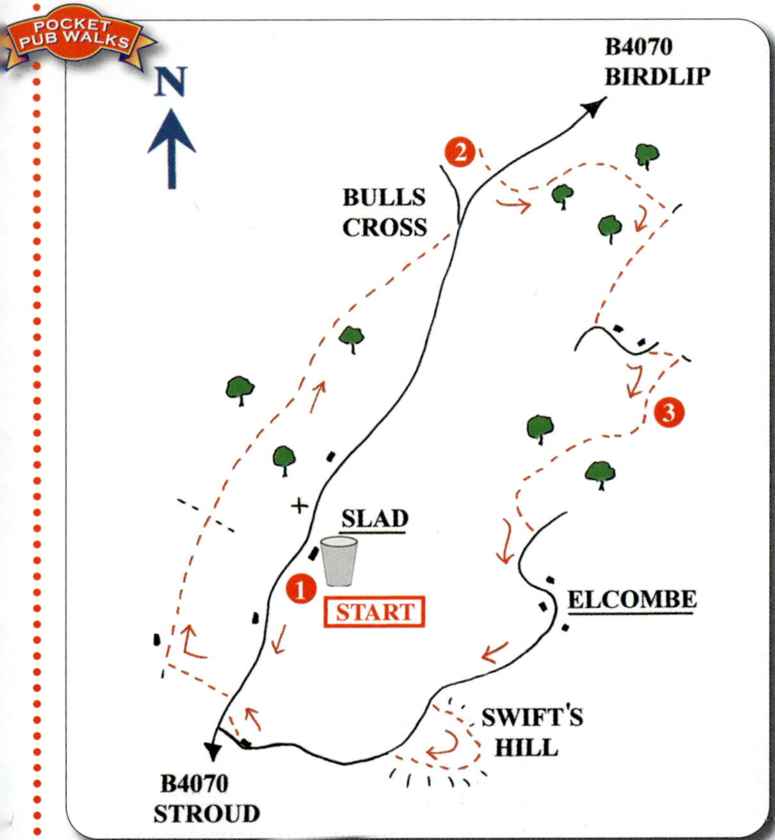

*The hamlet of Elcombe nestles in the valley*

directly ahead, initially through tree cover and then across an open field, continuing until it enters **Frith Wood Reserve**. Keep following the path ahead until in just over ½ mile it joins the B4070 at **Bulls Cross**. Follow the main road ahead for 100 yards to a point where a public footpath crosses the road.

2 Turn right and follow what is a track downhill through woodland. In 600 yards, in the bottom of a valley, follow a path on the right that passes a pond on the left before reaching a cross track. Keep ahead, climbing steeply uphill, to reach a track on the hilltop. Follow this track to the right to a gate, before continuing across an open hilltop to reach a junction. Take a sharp left turn along a private road and continue for 250 yards to a left-hand bend by **Snow's Farm**. At this point, pass through a gate on the right and follow a path diagonally to the left downhill to a stream. Cross this stream and a stile ahead, walk ahead a few paces into a field and veer right to a path that soon crosses another stream. Beyond the stream, cross a stile and follow a path ahead that climbs diagonally to the left to a gap in the hedgerow in the end field

boundary. Continue following this path as it climbs diagonally uphill to a stile at the entrance to **Catswood**.

3 Follow this path to the right and, ignoring a left and right turn along the way, continue for 600 yards to a fork, just beyond a point where a path comes in on the right. Take the right fork and continue to a junction. Turn right and follow a lane for 400 yards, passing the hamlet of **Elcombe**, to reach a cattle grid. Beyond this grid, turn left and follow a path onto **Elliot Nature Reserve** on **Swift's Hill**. Beyond a gate, keep on the path as it climbs steadily uphill before bearing right around the top of an old quarry to emerge onto an open hilltop. Walk across to the southern edge of the hilltop, with a good view towards Stroud ahead. Turn right and drop down the hillside to a cattle grid at the foot of the slope. Follow the lane ahead for 350 yards, ignoring a left turn along the way, to reach **Vatch Cottage** in the valley bottom. Just past this property, cross a stile on the right and follow a path up the right edge of a field to a stile and the B4070. Follow the road to the right back to the **Woolpack**.

## Places of interest nearby

**Stroud**, a few miles south of Slad, grew up on the steep hillsides at the junction of no fewer than five valleys. With water power everywhere, and sheep grazing on just about every hillside around the town, it was inevitable that it would become the pre-eminent centre of the Cotswold woollen industry. The town's **Museum in the Park** documents Stroud's rich and illustrious history. Housed in a Grade II, 17th-century wool merchant's mansion, the 5,000 exhibits range from dinosaur bones through to the world's first lawnmower and everything else in between. ☎ 01453 763394 or visit www.museuminthepark.org.uk for further information.

# 10 Sapperton

## *The Daneway Inn*

**An excellent circuit** in a corner of the Cotswolds that is justifiably popular with walkers. It explores the Upper Frome Valley above Stroud, where the decaying remains of the Thames & Severn Canal cut through the Cotswold plateau by means of the Sapperton Tunnel. This is an area of steep-sided wooded valleys, quite beautiful in the autumn when the name 'Golden Valley' will certainly ring true. Just occasionally, a view is afforded of the locality from some isolated vantage point, and quite dramatic and far ranging these views turn out to be too. Lovers of Cotswold architecture will find a great deal that catches the eye in the small village of Sapperton. St Kenhelm's church, with its Jacobean woodwork and stone monuments, is an absolute gem.

**Distance** – 3 miles.

**OS Explorer** 168 Stroud, Tetbury & Malmesbury.
GR SO939034.
A flat valley bottom, with some climbing onto the adjoining hillsides.

**Starting point** The Daneway Inn at Sapperton.

***How to get there*** *The Daneway Inn lies just below Sapperton village in a rather quiet corner of the Cotswolds. Sapperton is signposted from the A419 Cirencester to Stroud road. From the village, follow the minor road signposted to Edgeworth and Bisley. This passes the Daneway Inn which has its own car park. There is also roadside parking in the vicinity.*

THE PUB

Like many old pubs, the **Daneway** could tell a fascinating story. In the late 18th century, West Country and Derbyshire miners converged on the area to be employed on construction work on the nearby Sapperton Tunnel. At 3,817 yards long, the tunnel carried the Thames & Severn Canal through the Cotswold plateau. Lodgings were constructed for some of the miners in what is today the Daneway. With the opening of the canal, the inn then became a resting place for bargees, no doubt exhausted after 'legging it' through one of Britain's longest canal tunnels. Today, the handsome whitewashed building with its stone tiles sits alongside the now derelict canal bed, with harnesses and brasses in the bar areas, testimony to the days of towing horses. The Daneway serves traditional food that ranges from sandwiches and ploughman's through to beef and Guinness pie and Cumberland sausages.

1 Exit the car park, turn left and, having crossed the canal bed, follow a path on the left marked as the **Wysis Way**. Follow this path along the edge of a field before joining the bed of the canal. Follow the towpath along to the western entrance to the

*Opening times: Monday 11 am to 2.30 pm; Tuesday to Friday 11 am to 2.30 pm and 6.30 pm to 11 pm; Saturday 11 am to 3 pm and 6.30 pm to 11 pm; Sunday 11 am to 3 pm and 7 pm to 10.30 pm.*
*☎ 01285 760297; postcode: GL7 6LN; www.thedaneway.com*

**Sapperton Tunnel** before veering right onto a path that climbs up from the canal. Keep on this path as it bears left across the tunnel's parapet to reach a stile and hillside field. Head uphill across the field, veering right all the while, passing a prominent oak tree before reaching a gate at the top of the field. Ignoring this gate, continue walking along the top edge of the field to reach another handgate by **Sapperton church**.

2 Pass through this handgate, enter the churchyard ahead and walk up through an avenue of trees leading away from the church to reach a lane in **Sapperton**. Turn left and follow this lane as it winds its way downhill into a wooded valley bottom. In 200 yards, where the lane ends at a property, follow a footpath ahead

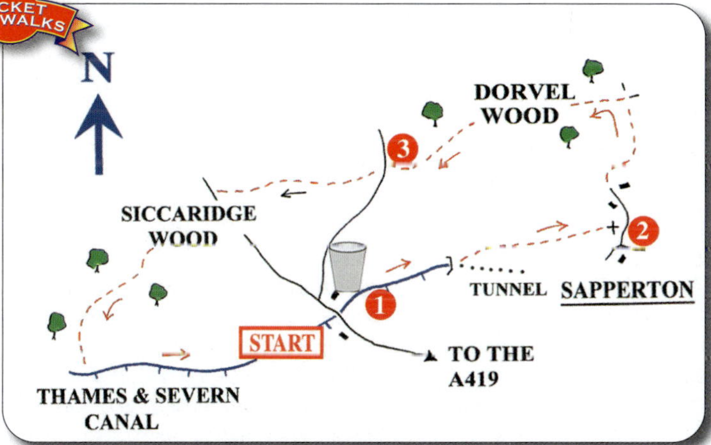

*One of the imposing monuments in St Kenelm's church*

that passes around the back of the property before reaching **Dorvel Bridge**. Cross this footbridge and keep on the path as it bears right and left to climb uphill through **Dorvel Wood**. At the first junction, take the left-hand path, which continues climbing uphill through the beech woodland. At a minor crossroads, keep ahead uphill for 50 yards to a more prominent crossroads on the hilltop. Turn left and follow the woodland path for 600 yards – it emerges onto open ground – before reaching a gate and lane.

3 Turn left for a few paces before crossing a pair of stiles on the right. Continue ahead along a path across open grassland – **Daneway Bank** – for 350 yards to a gate and lane. Cross to a gate opposite and enter **Siccaridge Wood Nature Reserve**. Follow the main woodland path ahead for ½ mile to a junction of paths. Follow the path ahead, which drops steeply downhill to reach **Whitehill Bridge** and the **Thames & Severn Canal**. Having crossed the bridge, turn left and follow the towpath ahead for ¾ mile back to the road and the **Daneway Inn**.

POCKET PUB WALKS

# 11 Between Nailsworth and Avening

## The Weighbridge Inn

**This walk explores** a delightful valley running west from Avening to Nailsworth, as well as climbing the valley side through the hamlet of Box to reach Minchinhampton, with its vast areas of open common land. Minchinhampton church has a strange stub of a spire, with the higher part of the structure being removed in 1863 for safety reasons. Below Minchinhampton lies Gatcombe Park, the beautiful spot where the political economist David Ricardo spent his last years before passing away in 1823. Tantalising glimpses of what is now best known for being the home of the Princess Royal can be had along the way. It is the fine natural landscape that will linger long in the memory, however – the steep wooded valley sides, coloured gold and

**Distance** – 6 miles.

**OS Explorer** 168 Stroud, Tetbury & Malmesbury. GR ST862993.
Steep hillsides and the flat open spaces of Minchinhampton Common.

**Starting point** The Weighbridge Inn.

***How to get there*** *The Weighbridge Inn lies on the B4014, midway between Nailsworth and Avening. There is a car park alongside the inn for patrons.*

yellow during the autumn, the open hilltops and the centuries-old sheep pasture that has yet to fall prey to the plough and arable farming.

The **Weighbridge** owes its name to the local woollen trade. Serving the nearby mills, raw materials were weighed as they entered the mills and the finished product weighed once again as it set out on its journeys to markets in places such as Bath, Bristol and London. The bar areas of the pub are delightfully old-fashioned, with stripped stone walls, antique settles, window seats and splendid open fireplaces. There is also a rather fine collection of black ironware, including sheep shears, gin traps, lamps and a collection of keys from a local mill. Perhaps the most popular option on the menu is the wonderful 2-in-1 pie. One half is a filling of your choice – maybe steak & mushroom or turkey & trimmings – the other half is delicious cauliflower cheese, all topped with melt-in-the-mouth pastry.

*Opening times on Monday to Saturday are 12 noon to 11 pm; on Sunday 12 noon to 10.30 pm.*
☎ *01453 832520; postcode: GL6 9AL; www.2in1pub.co.uk*

**1** Follow the lane opposite the **Weighbridge Inn** towards Minchinhampton and, in 100 yards, turn left along a path that leads to **Holcombe Glen**. Keep on the path running to the right of the property ahead. Continue along a woodland path to a track, cross and follow a path on uphill to a gap in a wall and a lane. Go over a stone stile opposite and continue following the path uphill, ignoring an early fork, for 300 yards to a stone stile and spring. Keep ahead, with a garden on the left, to a stile and lane by **Sweet Briar Cottage** in **Box**. Keep uphill to a junction, turn left to the next junction, keep left, passing **Clifton Cottage** on the right, and continue on uphill to a junction on **Minchinhampton Common** by the **Halfway House Inn**. Turn right, waymarked to Minchinhampton, initially passing the inn on the right. In 300 yards, by a wall and some conifers, turn left and follow the wall along the edge of the common. Keep following the wall in 400 yards as it bears right to meet a road by **Windmill Lodge**.

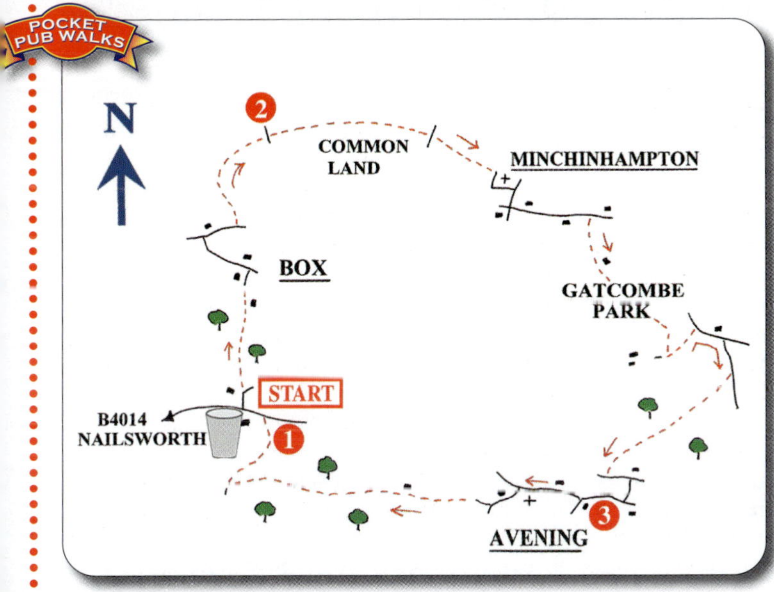

*The path to Avening*

2 Cross the road and follow the common opposite, making for a gabled property. Continue across the common beyond this property, a wall on the right, for 400 yards to the next road. Cross, and follow the line of the wall opposite across the common to reach a road by **Minchinhampton church**. Turn right and, at the next junction, left to the **High Street** by the **Crown Inn**. Turn right down to a crossroads then left along **Tetbury Street**. In 350 yards, cross a cattle grid before turning right in a few paces along a track. Where the track ends at a stable, keep ahead on a path down to a stile. Bear half-left across a field down to a gate and track before continuing uphill for ¼ mile to a junction by **Gatcombe Farm**. Turn left along a drive to a road, then right into **Hampton Fields**. Beyond a green and junction, keep ahead along a road for 300 yards to a track on the right, almost at the end of woodland. Turn right along what is called **Steps Lane** and follow

the track for ¾ mile to a junction in **Avening**. Turn left, passing a number of houses, to a junction in 400 yards. Turn right and, at the next junction, right along to the B4014 by the **Cross Inn**.

3 Follow the road ahead towards **Nailsworth** and, having passed the **Bell Inn** on the left and **Rectory Lane** on the right, turn left into a cul de sac called **Woodstock Lane**. In 150 yards, keep right at a fork and, in 100 yards, keep right at a junction along a bridleway. In 200 yards, ignore a left fork leading to a stable, keeping ahead instead along the main track to reach a gate. Cross an open field to a gateway and **Longman's Barn Farm**. Follow the path past the farm to a gate by a barn, keep ahead to another gate and then cross an open field to a gate at the entrance to **Hazel Wood**. Follow the footpath ahead for ¼ mile to the end of the wood, turn right to a handgate and bridleway and then left for 200 yards before following the track downhill to the right to reach an open field. Continue on downhill to the B4014 by **Iron Mills**, before turning left along to the **Weighbridge Inn**.

## Places of interest nearby

**Nailsworth** is a bustling little town on the A46, just a few miles west of the Weighbridge Inn. In recent years, it has developed a range of independent and unusual shops, ranging from delicatessens and bakeries to gift shops and art and craft stores. It is, for example, home to **Hobbs House Bakery**, one of the best bakeries in the country. Established in 1920, Hobbs House is a genuine family business with five generations of baking experience and the recipient of countless awards and accolades. There is also the **Rivers Gallery**, which specialises in a wide range of contemporary paintings, sculpture, ceramics, glass and turned wood. Visit the website www.nailsworth.com for further information.

POCKET PUB WALKS

# 12 Kingscote

## *Hunters Hall Inn*

**Kingscote and Hunters Hall** lie high on the Cotswold plateau, sitting astride the 700 ft contour line. Below Kingscote, however, this undulating landscape gives way to the Cotswold escarpment and its associated valleys in and around Wotton-under-Edge and Dursley. This walk explores a number of these marvellously secluded valleys, whose steep sides and damp marshy bottoms have prevented the march of the plough and its associated arable crops. Lengthy sections of this walk follow the tributary valleys that feed into Ozleworth Bottom. Ozleworth itself is a delight, with its grouping of grand mansion and ancient church. It has the only round churchyard in Gloucestershire, and the tower is the only six-sided tower in England that stands in the middle of a church. And nearby is

# Kingscote Walk 12

**Distance** – 6 miles.

**OS Explorer** 168 Stroud, Tetbury & Malmesbury.
GR ST814960.
Steep hillsides. The dense woodland cover and the streams that follow the valley floors mean that the going can be muddy underfoot at certain times of the year.

**Starting point** Hunters Hall Inn.

***How to get there*** *Hunters Hall Inn lies on the A4135 road between Dursley and Tetbury. There is a large car park at the rear for customers. Opposite the inn is a quiet side road leading into Kingscote itself where there is room for roadside parking.*

Newington Bagpath with its finely preserved motte, as well as the attractive grounds of Lasborough Park. The acres of ancient woodland make this a particularly fine seasonal excursion, with the red, yellow and gold colours of autumn being stunning.

THE PUB

**Hunters Hall Inn** is a building of great antiquity. The earliest record of this place was in 1604 when it comprised a house, an inn, stables and a blacksmith's shop. Early in the 20th century, entertainment and dances were held above the stables, with this record of hospitality continuing to this day. The inn has a wealth of charm and character, with stone-flagged floors, blackened beams, vast stone hearths, ancient cast-iron fire baskets and assorted artefacts, including stuffed animals in their glass cases and shooting prints. The menu ranges from sandwiches upwards, with a particular favourite being the house deli board. Chiltern-cured ham, roast chicken breast and Shropshire blue cheese come complete with delicious crusty bread and accompaniments such as piccalilli and onion marmalade.

*Hunters Hall is open all day and every day. Food in various formats is served from 12 noon right through until 10 pm, whilst early arrivals can enjoy breakfast between 8 am and 12 noon.*
☎ *01453 860393; postcode: GL8 8XZ; www.huntershallinn.co.uk*

1 With your back to the inn and facing the main road, turn right then very shortly right again to **Bagpath**. In ½ mile at a junction, keep ahead in the direction of Bagpath. In 300 yards, at the next junction, keep left to Bagpath. In just a few paces, turn right along an unmarked lane. Follow this lane as it drops down into – and up out of – a valley, before continuing across the level hilltop for ¼ mile to a waymarked footpath on the left. Follow what is a driveway across to **Sawcombe Farm**. Having passed a barn on the right, keep on the track beyond a gateway that bears right into a field. Follow the right edge of the field, with a wooded bank on the right, pass through a gap in the hedge at the end of the field and walk the length of a second field to a gateway. Beyond this gateway, walk across to a handgate in the middle of the end field boundary ahead. Follow the right edge of the next field to a stile in the corner of the field, before following a footpath that swings right to a gate and stile. Follow the left edge of the next field to a gate and stile and lane. Turn left and, in 100 yards, where the lane bears right, keep ahead along a gated path to **Ozleworth church**. On reaching a tarmac drive, turn left towards the church. In 100 yards, detour right to the church – for the main walk, keep ahead along a bridlepath.

2 Follow this path as it winds its way through a riding complex to reach a crossroads of paths. Follow the path ahead that drops downhill through a belt of trees to a cattle grid. Follow a broad path that bears right down through this hillside field and keep on this path as it swings left and drops downhill into a valley bottom. In the valley bottom, keep on the path as it bears sharply right and crosses a small stream. Follow this broad path along the opposite

side of the valley for 75 yards before veering right to follow the course of **Marles Brook** across a long field, with the stream in the tree cover on the right. In the far right corner of the field, pass through a gateway, cross a stream on the right, join a track and

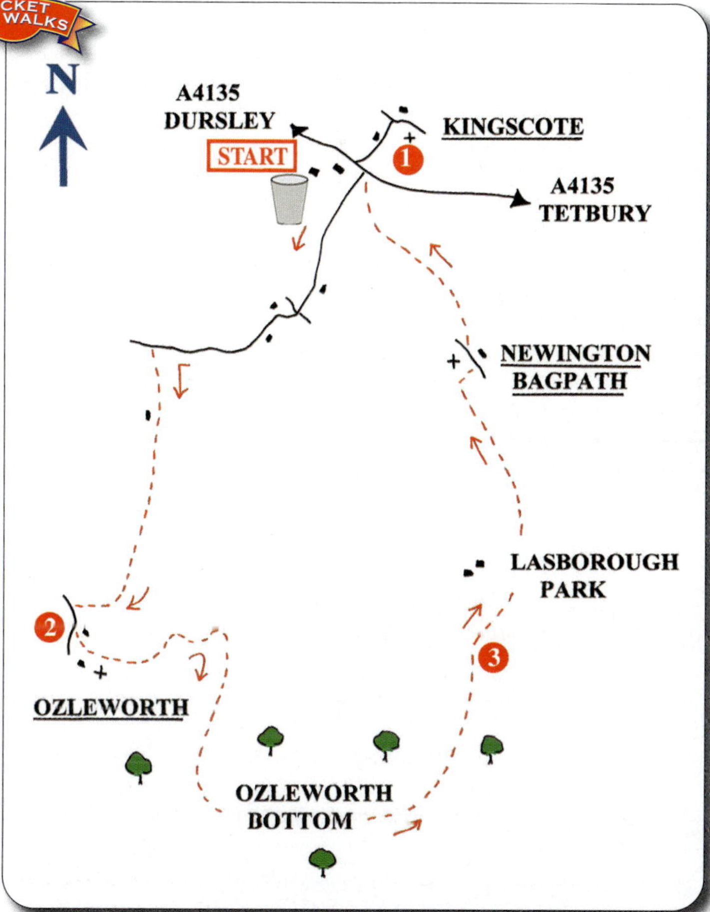

turn left. In 75 yards, at a junction, turn left and follow a path into **Ozleworth Bottom**, initially crossing a footbridge. In just over ½ mile, where the track bears left out of the valley bottom, keep ahead through a gap in the trees to an area of wetland. Follow a path along the left edge of what is a pond and continue through dense woodland for ¼ mile to a footbridge. Continue uphill to another pond and follow a path along its right edge and on uphill to a gate and open parkland. Follow a grassy path ahead for 350 yards to a gate and cattle grid.

3 Walk ahead to a marker post before going uphill towards the end of a belt of woodland. On the hilltop, continue walking along to the end of the field to a gate in the end wall, 100 yards down from the corner of the field. Walk ahead across the next field to a motte, before bearing right down to a gate and lane, with an old church in the trees on the left. Follow the lane to the left and, once past the church, pass through a gateway on the right and follow the right edge of a field for 150 yards to a gate on the right. Beyond this gate, follow a woodland path down to a gate and hillside field. Walk across to the left-hand field boundary and follow it to the right up to a gate. Beyond this gate, follow the right edge of a field to the next gate and continue along a path up to an arable field just past beech trees. Follow the left edge of this field to a gate in its far left corner and the main road by **Hunters Hall Inn**.

## Places of interest nearby

For lovers of antiques, a visit to **Tetbury** is a must. There are well over a dozen antique shops. Other attractions in the town include the **Police Bygones Museum**, the 17th-century **Market House** and **St Mary's church**, built in the Gothic style in 1781. Visit www.visittetbury.co.uk for more information on Tetbury.

POCKET PUB WALKS

# 13 Hillesley

## *The Fleece Inn*

**Geologists use the term** 'escarpment' but the colloquial phrase is 'Cotswold Edge'. This is where the high wolds come tumbling down to the flat open expanses of the Severn Vale. Hillesley lies quite literally on the edge. To the west is the Severn Estuary and the distant Welsh hills, whilst behind the village a steep slope leads up to the region's high ground. This walk explores this most beautiful of landscapes with open views being just one of the highlights along the way. There is also Hawkesbury, with its 'almost cathedral-like' church, the hidden delights of the remote and picturesque Kilcott Valley and the ancient woodlands in and around Hennel Bottom. This is quite simply a delightful pastoral excursion deep in the southern Cotswolds.

**Distance** – 6 miles.

**OS Explorer** 167 Thornbury, Dursley & Yate. GR ST769896. Some not insignificant climbs on the Cotswold escarpment; open hilltops and sheltered valleys.

**Starting point** The Fleece Inn, Hillesley.

***How to get there*** *The hamlet of Dunkirk lies 15 miles north of Bath, on the A46. Follow the unclassified road signposted to Hawkesbury Upton from this point. Continue through Hawkesbury Upton and on to Hillesley, the next village, where the Fleece has a prominent location. Park at the inn or on the roadside nearby.*

The **Fleece Inn** is a handsome whitewashed building with a fine Cotswold stone roof. The name, of course, reflects sheep farming, which was the staple industry in this region in bygone days. The bar areas, with their beams and stripped tables, prints and open fireplaces, give a relaxing feel to what is a very popular inn. Equally important, the food is excellent as well. Whether you fancy something light such as a ploughman's or sandwiches, or a more substantial meal that includes locally-sourced meat and vegetables, you will not be disappointed. To quote from the publicity blurb 'a traditional country inn with a twist'.

*Opening times are 12 noon to 3 pm and 6 pm to 10.30 pm.*
*☎ 01453 843189; postcode: GL12 7RQ;*
*www.thefleeceinnhillesley.com*

1 With your back to the **Fleece Inn**, follow **Chapel Lane** to the left. Where this lane bears left by **Albany Cottage**, keep ahead to a

gate and stile. Walk up the left edge of the field ahead to a gate before following an enclosed path on uphill – it soon passes through woodland – to emerge into an open hilltop field. Keep ahead for a short distance before turning right through a gap in the hedge. Walk along the edge of the woodland before following the left edge of a hilltop field towards a barn conversion. Cross a

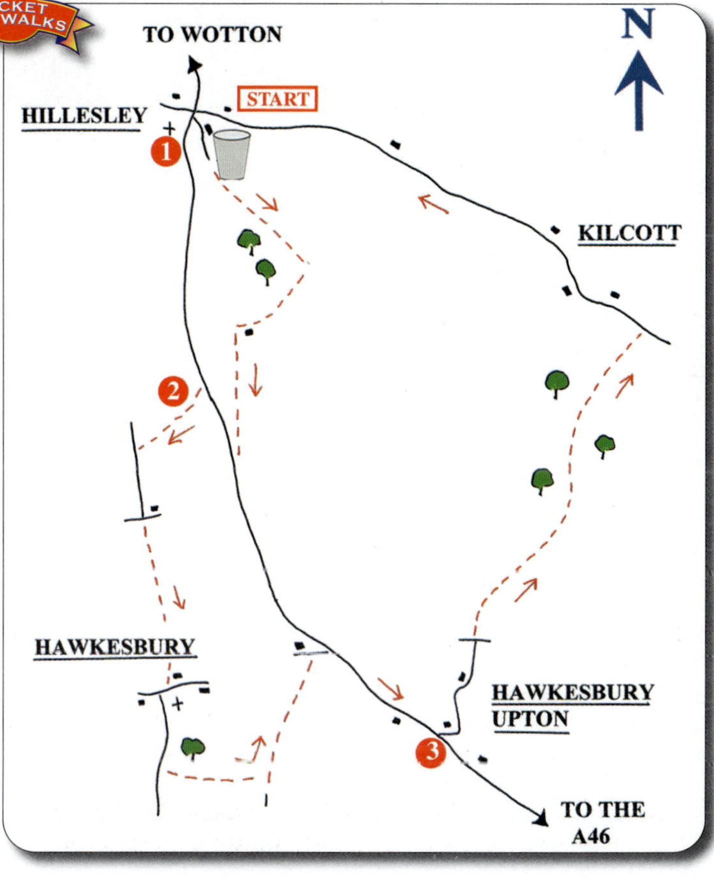

*One of the locals having a paddle*

stile on the far side of the field. Walk along in front of the barn and then follow a drive to the left for ½ mile to reach the Hawkesbury Upton to Wotton road. Turn right and, in 300 yards, where the road bears right and begins to drop downhill, follow a footpath on the left through a gateway to a fine viewpoint.

2 Walk across the top of the field ahead to the second of two handgates on the left. Pass through this gateway into a field, turn right and follow the right edge of the field for 250 yards to a stile half-concealed in the hedgerow. Drop down to a second stile and cross the field ahead to a stile in the opposite field boundary. Join a lane, turn left and walk along to a crossroads in 200 yards. Follow the gated byway opposite for ½ mile through to a gate and the road in **Hawkesbury** by the church. Turn right and, in 100 yards, turn left towards **Horton**. In 200 yards, turn left onto a gated track – waymarked as a public footpath. Follow this track uphill to a gate, before following the left edges of two fields to reach the **Cotswold Way**. Follow this broad track to the left for 250 yards to its junction with a lane. Turn right up to the main road in

**Hawkesbury Upton** by the **Drover's Pool** and follow this road to the right through the village to a junction by the war memorial.

3 Bear left into **Back Street** and follow this road as it winds its way out of **Hawkesbury Upton** to reach a junction in 300 yards. Follow the footpath opposite, which drops downhill through some tree cover to reach a gate and hillside field. Walk ahead across this field, dropping gently downhill, to reach a gate in the end field boundary. Continue in the same direction across the next field to reach a gap in the end field boundary. Keep ahead in the next field to reach a gate to the left of a water trough, before dropping downhill to cross a footbridge over a stream in the valley bottom. Turn right and continue through the valley to reach a gate and woodland. Follow the main ride ahead through the woodland for 250 yards to a junction of paths. Keep ahead along the main ride to reach a gate and the lane that runs through the **Kilcott Valley**. Follow this lane for 1½ miles to its junction with the main road in **Hillesley**. Turn left and, in a few paces, keep ahead into **Chapel Lane** to return to the **Fleece Inn**.

## Places of interest nearby

**Wotton-under-Edge** is a charming market town just a few miles north of Hillesley. Its reputation is built upon its wide range of independent shops, something of a rarity in today's all too ubiquitous world of High Street chains. **Newark Park**, a National Trust property just outside the town, is well worth a visit. From its Tudor origins to today, Newark Park contains elements reflecting 450 years of history. The atmospheric house is lived in and is furnished with an eclectic mix of old and modern. Outside, the wild romantic garden and landscape, with fantastic views to the distant Mendip Hills, are breathtaking. ☎ 01793 817666 for details of opening days and times.

POCKET PUB WALKS

# 14 Marshfield

## *The Catherine Wheel*

**Marshfield enjoys a** hilltop location high on the Cotswold plateau. The main street runs for close on half a mile from the Georgian tollhouse at its western end through to the grouping of church and manor house at its eastern end. Almost every residence in the High Street is well over 100 years old, many significantly older, with the finest frontage being arguably that of the Catherine Wheel inn. The walk descends into St Catherine's Valley with stunning vistas at every turn, before climbing up to Cold Ashton, another hilltop settlement. Here the ancient manor house will catch the eye, as will the attractive church. A vast swathe of unimproved limestone grassland, mainly

**Distance** – 6 miles.

**OS Explorer** 155 Bristol & Bath. GR ST779738.
Field paths, lanes and tracks, with potentially muddy valley bottoms and steep hillsides.

**Starting point** The Catherine Wheel in Marshfield's High Street.

***How to get there*** *Marshfield lies just off of the A420 between Bristol and Chippenham. Follow the signs into the village from the main road and the Catherine Wheel fronts onto the High Street at the eastern end of the village. Parking is available on the High Street where there are no restrictions.*

access land, marks the return to Marshfield. With the path running through a valley bottom surrounded by steep hillsides, the landscape is simply quite stunning.

THE PUB

With its exposed stonework and motley collection of settles, chairs and stripped tables, there is a real traditional atmosphere at the **Catherine Wheel**. The rear bar has a cottage-like feel whilst the more formal dining room is Georgian in character with a rather grand fireplace. The lunch menu offers plenty of choice ranging from staples such as sandwiches, steak & kidney pie and jacket potatoes, through to such tempting options as smoked haddock, Scotch eggs and spinach & feta filo pie with a Greek salad. There are fine beers from the nearby Cotswold Spring Brewery, too.

*Opening times are all day, every day, with food served from 12 noon to 2 pm and 6.30 pm to 9 pm.*
☎ *01225 892220; postcode: SN14 8LR; www.thecatherinewheel.co.uk*

1 With your back to the **Catherine Wheel**, follow the **High Street** to the left for 100 yards before turning left into **Sheepfair Lane**. In 300 yards, at a junction, turn left. In 150 yards, turn right into a cul de sac called **Beeks Lane**. In ½ mile, turn left onto a public bridleway. In 300 yards, cross a stile alongside a gate on the right. Walk along the top right edge of the field ahead to reach a handgate in the corner of the field. Beyond this handgate, turn left down the edge of the next field before turning right to follow the lower field boundary. In the corner of the field, cross a stile and continue walking along the left edge of the following field. In the corner of the field, veer left down to a stile, cross a track and go over another stile opposite. Bear half-right across the field ahead over to a stile in the right-hand field boundary and a good view of **St Catherine's Valley**. Drop downhill across a hillside field to a pair of stiles in the bottom right-hand corner of the field. Cross these stiles and follow a field path through the valley

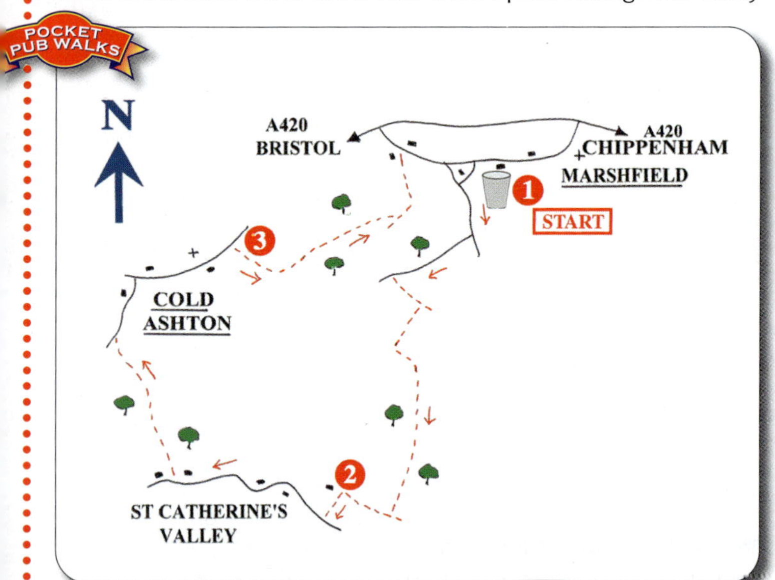

*The manor house in Cold Ashton*

bottom across two fields to reach an unmetalled driveway by a property.

2 Follow this driveway to the left up to the lane running through **St Catherine's Valley**. Walk along this lane to the right uphill out of the valley for 600 yards to reach **Fry's Farm**. Turn right onto a track that runs between the farmhouse and a barn. Follow this track for 350 yards to a gate before walking across to a gate in the far left corner of the field ahead by a solitary ash tree. Beyond this gate, follow the left edge of the next field to its corner before turning right to walk up the end field boundary to reach a gateway and lane. Follow the lane to the right up to a road junction in Cold Ashton, turn right and walk through the village. Some 100 yards past the last property on the right in **Cold Ashton**, turn right at a gateway to follow a waymarked footpath.

3 Walk down the left edge of the field ahead before walking down the left edge of a second field to a gate partway down the field. Pass through this gateway and follow a sunken path ahead downhill towards the valley bottom. On reaching a gate, continue following the path downhill, with a fence on the right. Keep following this path as it bears left across the bottom of the field. Continue walking through the valley, maintaining the same direction – this is access land – until the field boundary on the right ends. Keep walking ahead through the valley just above the valley bottom to reach a handgate in ½ mile in the corner of the field. Continue ahead through the valley, with a small stream on the right, to reach a stile. Continue ahead through the valley bottom until the path approaches a gate, with a fence coming down from the right. At this point, veer right up to a stile at the top of the field and join a track. Follow this track, which soon bears left, all the way up to the western end of the **High Street** in **Marshfield** by a former toll house. Turn right, and follow the High Street for 500 yards back to the **Catherine Wheel**.

## Place of interest nearby

**Dyrham House and Park** are just a ten-minute drive from Marshfield. This fine William and Mary house, set in 265 acres of ancient deer park, was built between 1691 and 1702 for William Blathwayt, William III's Secretary of State and Secretary at War. The rooms have changed little since they were furnished by Blathwayt in the Dutch style with Delft china, Dutch paintings and fine 17th-century textiles. For full details on the opening times of this National Trust property, visit www.nationaltrust.org.uk and search for Dyrham Park or ☎ 0117 937 2501.

POCKET PUB WALKS

# 15 Avoncliff

## *The Cross Guns*

**In recent years**, the Cotswolds Area of Outstanding Natural Beauty has been extended in a southerly direction to encompass the Avon Valley between Bath and Bradford-on-Avon. This is very much a natural extension, with the underlying bedrock being the rich and golden limestone that provided the building blocks for so many of the local properties. Between Avoncliff and Bradford-on-Avon lies a watery paradise bounded by the River Avon and the Kennet & Avon Canal. Bradford, with its Saxon church, Town Bridge, ancient lock-up and ranks of weavers' cottages is a delight. Avoncliff is much the same – a diminutive hamlet deep in the Avon Valley dominated by a vast aqueduct that carries the canal across the Avon. This is a walk that is understandably one of the most popular in the region.

**Distance** – 3½ miles.

**OS Explorer** 156 Chippenham & Bradford-on-Avon.
GR ST825607.
Level paths alongside the River Avon and the Kennet & Avon Canal, with just one short climb up to the canal from the river.

**Starting point** The pay & display station car park in Bradford-on-Avon. Note: Because of limited parking and difficult access to Avoncliff, this walk visits the Cross Guns pub halfway around the circuit.

***How to get there*** *Leave the A4 at Bathford just to the east of Bath and follow the A363 into the centre of Bradford-on-Avon. Having crossed the Town Bridge over the River Avon, turn right in 100 yards at a mini-roundabout into the station car park.*

THE PUB

The **Cross Guns** is a gem. Dating back to the 17th century, it was frequented by local weavers before it became a bargees' watering hole with the arrival of the K&A Canal. It is a marvellously old-fashioned pub with a vast stone fireplace, stone walls, low beams and solid oak tables. The best spot to rest and linger awhile is on the delightful terrace that drops down to the banks of the Avon. There can be few more pleasant locations in which to enjoy a pint of one of the fine ales from the nearby Box Steam Brewery, as well as the delicious home-made food that includes a garden menu, light bites and a more substantial restaurant menu.

*Opening times are all day, every day from 10 am to 11 pm. Food is served from 12 noon until 9 pm.*
☎ *01225 862335; postcode: BA15 2HB; www.crossguns.net*

1 Walk to the far end of the station car park before following a path that drops downhill to the left, passing underneath a railway bridge and joining the banks of the **River Avon**. Continue along this path as it crosses a recreational area before joining a tarmac path, with the old buildings of **Barton Farm** on the left and a packhorse bridge on the right. Follow this path, with the **Avon** on the right, for just under ½ mile to where it veers left uphill towards the **K&A Canal**. At this point, veer right and continue following a path alongside the Avon to reach a gateway and open field. Follow the obvious field path ahead across four fields, all the while bordering the river.

2 At the far side of the fourth field, turn left and follow a stepped path up to the **K&A** towpath. Turn right into **Avoncliff** where, just before the aqueduct, a right turn brings you to the **Cross Guns**. Return to the canal and turn left, following the towpath back towards **Bradford-on-Avon**. In 1 mile, just before Bradford's tithe barn, take a path on the left downhill back to the riverside path followed at the outset. Follow this path to the right back across the grassy recreational area and under the railway bridge to return to the station car park.

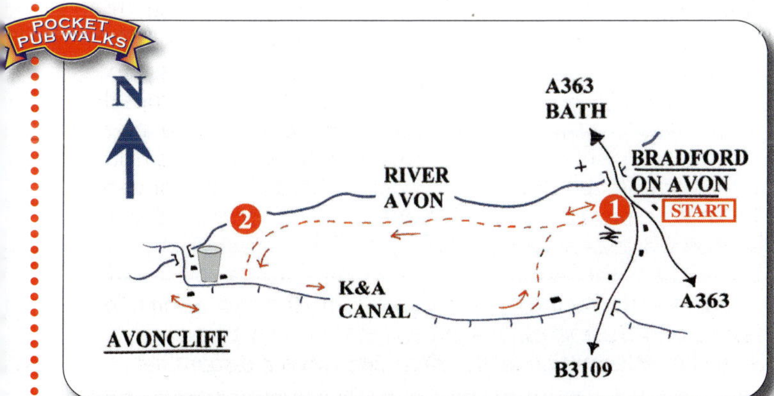

*The magnificent River Avon*

## Places of interest nearby

There are three fine National Trust properties within a short distance of Bradford-on-Avon. To the east is **Courts Garden** in Holt, whilst in nearby **Great Chalfield** is a delightful manor house and garden, enhanced by a moat and gatehouse. To the south-west of Bradford, at **Westwood** is another manor house, dating from the 15th century and with splendid Gothic and Jacobean windows. Both Great Chalfield and Westwood also have interesting churches, the former small in scale with stained glass showing the parable of the sower, the latter of the grand Perpendicular design. Visit www.nationaltrust.org.uk for further information.